D1544261

POWERFUL LONG LADDER

POWERFUL

LONG LADDER

BY OWEN DODSON

"It take a powerful long ladder to climb to the sky
An catch the bird of freedom for the dark."

FARRAR, STRAUS AND GIROUX

New York

TO MY SISTERS:

LILLIAN AND EDITH

WITH LOVE

Thanks are due to *The Answer, Christendom, Common Ground, The Crisis, Mademoiselle, The Negro Caravan, Negro Quarterly, Opportunity, Phylon, Theatre Arts, Tomorrow,* and *View* for their kind permission to reprint poems in this book.

CONTENTS

POWERFUL LONG LADDER

LAMENT

Wake up, boy, and tell me how you died:
What sense was alert last,
What immediate intuition about us
You clutched like a bullet when your nails
Dug red in your yellow palm
And that map the fortunetellers read
(this line for money, this for love)
Childish again and smeared.

the Mississippi drank itself one night,
the bridge from which you hung threw its arms up,
folded into mud like an old obscene accordion,
the crowd dispersed
counted on its fingers one by one

Wake up, boy, I go to death tomorrow,
Tell me what road you took,
What hour in the day is luckiest,
Did your Adam's apple explode?
Who sewed stitches in your angry heart?
O wake . . .
I here give up my soul.
Wake up . . .
And deliver love to mud for everlasting evermore.
Wake . . .
I here give up all nature including grass,
The second crocus, the cotton stem with the dry head.
Wake up, wake, I go . . .
Must I here give you up, my friend,

To wander where I wander to barbed wire crossed at intervals
     like Evil stars?

Save me!
Tell me the acrostic, the cross, the crown or the fire . . .
O, wake up, wake!

GUITAR

Ma six string guitar with the lonesome sound
Can't hold its own against a Georgia hound.

O mamma when the sun goes the downstairs way
And the night spreads out an the moon make day,

I sits with ma feet raised to the rail
And sings the song bout ma buddy in jail:

> *In the red-dirt land,*
> *And the pine tree high,*
> *Gonna find me peace*
> *By-an-by.*
>
> *Gonna find me a baby*
> *Some pretty-eye gal*
> *To be ma mother*
> *Ma wife an pal.*
>
> *Ain't had nobody*
> *To call me home*
> *From the electric cities*
> *Where I roam.*
>
> *Yes, I been travelin*
> *Over all*
> *To find a place*
> *What I could call*
> *Home, baby,*
> *Sweet cotton-field home. . . .*

When I gets to the place where a cracker got mad,
Struck ma fine buddy, struck all I had,
The hound start howlin till the stars break down
An make ma song like a boat what's drown.

Ma six string guitar with the lonesome sound
Can't hold its own against that Georgia hound.

SORROW IS THE ONLY FAITHFUL ONE

Sorrow is the only faithful one:
The lone companion clinging like a season
To its original skin no matter what the variations.

If all the mountains paraded
Eating the valleys as they went
And the sun were a coiffure on the highest peak,

Sorrow would be there between
The sparkling and the giant laughter
Of the enemy when the clouds come down to swim.

But I am less, unmagic, black,
Sorrow clings to me more than to doomsday mountains
Or erosion scars on a palisade.

Sorrow has a song like a leech
Crying because the sand's blood is dry
And the stars reflected in the lake

Are water for all their twinkling
And bloodless for all their charm.
I have blood, and a song.

Sorrow is the only faithful one.

7

BLACK MOTHER PRAYING

My great God, You been a tenderness to me,
Through the thick and through the thin;
You been a pilla to my soul;
You been like the shinin light a mornin in the black dark,
A elevator to my spirit.

Now there's a fire in this land like a last judgment,
And I done sat down by the rivers of Babylon
And wept deep when I remembered Zion,
Seein the water that can't quench fire
And the fire that burn up rivers.
Lord, I'm gonna say my say real quick and simple:

You know bout this war that's bitin the skies and gougin out the earth.
Last month, Lord, I bid my last boy away to fight.
I got all my boys fightin now for they country.
Didn't think bout it cept it were for freedom;
Didn't think cause they was black they wasn't American;
Didn't think a thing cept that they was my only sons,
And there was mothers all over the world
Sacrificin they sons like You let Yours be nailed
To the wood for men to behold the right.

Now I'm a black mother, Lord, I knows that now,
Black and burnin in these burnin times.
I can't hold my peace cause peace ain't fit to mention
When they's fightin right here in our streets
Like dogs—mongrel dogs and hill cats.
White is fightin black right here where hate abides like a cancer wound

And Freedom is writ big and crossed out:
Where, bless God, they's draggin us outta cars
In Texas and California, in Newark, Detroit,

Blood on the darkness, Lord, blood on the pavement,
Leavin us moanin and afraid.
What has we done?
Where and when has we done?
They's plantin the seeds of hate down in our bone marrow
When we don't want to hate.

We don't speak much in the street where I live, my God,
Nobody speak much, but we thinkin deep
Of the black sons in lands far as the wind can go,
Black boys fightin this war with them.

We thinkin deep bout they sisters stitchin airplane canvas,
And they old fathers plowin for wheat,
And they mothers bendin over washtubs,
They brothers at the factory wheels:
They all is bein body beat and spirit beat and heart sore and wonderin.

Listen, Lord, they ain't nowhere for black mothers to turn.
Won't You plant Your Son's goodness in this land
Before it too late?
Set Your stars of sweetness twinklin over us like winda lamps
Before it too late?
Help these men to see they losin while they winnin
Long as they allow theyselves to lynch in the city streets and
            on country roads?

When can I pray again,
View peace in my own parlor again?
When my sons come home
How can I show em my broken hands?

How can I show em they sister's twisted back?
How can I present they land to them?
How, when they been battlin in far places for freedom?
Better let em die in the desert drinkin sand
Or holdin onto water and shippin into death
Than they come back an see they sufferin for vain.

I done seen a man runnin for his life,
Runnin like the wind from a mob, to no shelter.
Where were a hidin place for him?
Saw a dark girl nine years old
Cryin cause her father done had
The light scratched from his eyes in the month of June.
Where the seein place for him?
A black boy lyin with his arms huggin the pavement in pain.
What he starin at?
Good people hands up, searched for guns and razors and pipes.
When they gonna pray again?

How, precious God, can I watch my son's eyes
When they hear this terrible?
How can I pray again when my tongue
Is near cleavin to the roof of my mouth?
Tell me, Lord, how?

Every time they strike us, they strikin Your Son;
Every time they shove us in, they cornerin they own children.
I'm gonna scream before I hope again.
I ain't never gonna hush my mouth or lay down this heavy, black,
          weary, terrible load
Until I fights to stamp my feet with my black sons
On a freedom solid rock and stand there peaceful
And look out into the star wilderness of the sky
And the land lyin about clean, and secure land,
And people not afraid again.

Lord, let us all see the golden wheat together,
Harvest the harvest together,
Touch the fulness and the hallelujah together.
                                    Amen.

EPITAPH FOR A NEGRO WOMAN

(*For Mary Paschall*)

How cool beneath this stone the soft moss lies,
How smooth and long the silken threads have kept
Without the taste of slender rain or stars,
How tranquilly the outer coats have slept.

Alone with only wind, with only ice,
The moss is growing, clinging to the stone;
And seeing only what the darkness shows,
It thrives without the moon, it thrives alone.

THE SIGNIFYING DARKNESS

There was an evil darkness way before
The war rose clear, a darkness before that dawn,
Before that midnight and that evening dusk:
A signifying darkness too few saw

When there was blazing light unfree
Of sun and unblown candle or artificial;
The darkness of skin and shame in it,
The darkness of condescension, greed and charity.

O, could you watch this map of prejudice:
How sharp the acid rivers eat,
The valleys deplore, the mountains scorn—
Then you would see Paris and Metz as victories less

For all their wide appeal and joy.
You would see here the black wet face
Of a dark mother staring at the blood
Ruin dust and bone and dead that was her boy.

PEARL PRIMUS

Who dances?
Is it the earth, the dark world underneath
Moving up, the goddess and her daughter
Dancing again, weaving their dance
Through the lines of corn, dancing
Through the vines with the grapes of wrath?
O, the sun is like a shawl on their backs,
The memory of stars halfway in their eyes.

Is it the memory of a lonely black boy lonely on a tree,
The black hope blaring ripeness under the tree,
Trumpeting up a lost and lonely Spring?

Is it Proserpine up again and longing
Or rivers of sweat forming men and growing?
This strangeness is an ease to me,
A refuge in the pop-eyed noon.

Is it Cassandra as she saw the dark wolf
And caught him fast and dug her prophetic fingernails
To below the hair into the flesh
Feeling a dark blood world of hate?

Who dances here?
Surely it is the black girl who has seen the vision,
Who waits, pistoning her feet in the air,
For the new world and the fruit of it?

POEM FOR PEARL'S DANCERS

SCENE: A SLAVE AUCTION

On my back they've written history, Lord,
On my back they've lashed out hell.

> My eyes run blood,
> The faces I see are blood,
> My toes can't dig no deeper in the dirt.

When my children get to reading, Lord,
On my back they'll read my tale.

> My lips taste blood,
> And in they souls they's blood.
> My tongue can't joy no future in this blood.

When my children get to shouting, Lord,
All around they'll shout this scene.

When my children get to manhood, Lord,
When my children get to standing straight,
Lord, Lord, Lord,
When that time come rolling down!

SOMEDAY WE'RE GONNA TEAR THEM PILLARS DOWN

(*For William Stanley Braithwaite*)

SLAVES:
We stir the unwarmin fire of slavery,
We dig in a sorry earth,
We dream terrible in a dark mornin,
Shiver in a burnin-hot afternoon,
Sleep in a tremblin night.
Fear sits on the cabins an sings a poison song.

ONE:
We wants the air to be clean,
Scrubbed cleaner than a windin sheet.

ANOTHER:
We wants hope to hover over while we sleep.

ONE: *Whispering*
Fear sits on the cabins singin his poison song . . .

A WOMAN:
They took ma strong-muscle John and cut his manhood off
An peeled the sight from his eyes,
An now he wander blind like blind Samson in Gaza,
Stumblin between the pillars of the big house,
An the pillars stay fixed in they place.
Someday he gonna pull them pillars down.

SLAVES:
When will the pillars crack an rock, break apart an terror the house?
When will the smoke blow outta the air?

ONE:

Never no more till the nostrils of fear
Smell the sweetness of freedom an the poison songs is only graveyard
    hummin.

SLAVE:

Where is freedom wanderin?
He do not knock at the door at night;
He do not sing in the burden-hot afternoon;
He do not wander here a-tall.

ONE:

Ma father say: Freedom a story they tell that never happen.

ANOTHER:

In the well when I looked down good I saw Freedom glancin up.
His face were shinin like a wisdom star
An he winked at me, he beckoned with his hands.

OLD ONE:

Death is in the well—
Never drink no more.
Death has a new kinda face—
Never look no more!

ONE:

When, O when, ma brothers, ma sisters, will the well be drained of
    masqueradin death?

ANOTHER:

When will the noosed rope strangle the nooser?
When will the whip turn snake an bite the holder?

SLAVE:

When will the pillars rock an crack, break apart an terror the house?
When will the smoke blow outta the air?
When, ma lonesome Jesus, when?

ONE:
When will freedom come whistlin up the road an knock at the door at
     night
An enter like a brother long gone, long lost?

SLAVES:
When, ma heartbroken Jesus, when?

ONE:
When will the pillars—

ANOTHER:
Samson—lock your arms about the pillars!

A MAN:
Mourn ya mournin in ya sleep at night,
Chew ya pain in the cellar.
In ma heart a secret is restin.
I'm gonna be free as the sky.
I been mendin horses' shoes for long.
I got money in the white folks' bank in Massa's name.
I been workin in the lonesome night after the lonesome day,
An I been secin the dawn spring up like a miracle bird.
I'm gonna buy me Freedom an mend Freedom's shoes an he can wander
     free.

SLAVES: *Laughing*
Ya gonna discover one of these days
That the white man got two dozen ways to lie an cheat
To conjure with deceit.

GIRL:
If I was blind I'd see a-plenty more than I see now.
I'd dream if I was blind; now I can't dream no more.

THE MAN:
I been seein the dawn spring up like a miracle bird.

WOMAN:
Someday, Lawd, someday
We gonna view a new-shinin light
Rise up like a bird in the dawn
An spread his wings on the dawnin sky.

A MAN:
It take a powerful long ladder to climb to the sky
An catch the bird of freedom for the dark.
Yes, it take a long climb.

SLAVES:
Lawd, it take a long long rope of years.

MEN:
It take a powerful hammer ta drive a long nail;
It take a powerful figurin to figure
How to build a strong tower on a puny sand.

SLAVES:
Lawd, it take a long long rope of years.

WOMEN:
Build us a tower of Freedom an catch the bird of freedom.

THE LEADER:
No hands can build Freedom but your own hands,
No strength can cancel it but your own strength.
But the bird, see it but never try to snare it.
Let it hover over. It is not a vulture bird.

SLAVES:

Seems like we heard that talkin some time long ago—lost—
But we remember—

THE LEADER:

Remember again.
In this wilderness your souls are bitter,
Your blood's not flowing free and smooth,
Your bodies are blistered like sin,
Your prayers are the prayers of a conquered wailing people
Who are praying for the evening light of Jesus.
O walk in the morning light,
Pray like standing-up men.
Let yourselves be yourselves,
Rise up and grasp the stones one by one
And never tire till the tower is done.
Sneak with me to the freedom place;
You'll never have to sneak no more
When you get there and sing the wonderful singing:

> *this sky is mine,*
> *these eyes are mine, truly mine,*
> *these twisted strong hands,*
> *this song flowing and the fruit of it,*
> *this dark heart,*
> *these children,*
> *this earth,*
> *are mine.*

SLAVES:

All are ours!

THE LEADER:

Will you go with me and suffer and sing our songs to the wilderness as
you pass?
In the night you'll hear the rats eating the seeds of time.
Women will die with the dream hovering over, whispering.

SLAVES:

Will it be freedom forever?
Tell us the fulsome story,
The whole plan, the whole pain.
When we get to the cold north country
Will freedom be warmin forever,
His tower built forever,
His bird forever an everlastin ever?

THE LEADER:

When you arrive you'll have to hold fast
And fight to keep your tower built stone by stone
With sweat and death and wilted hope made strong.
You'll never keep it unless you keep it.
You're sheltered here but in the cold places only your heart will keep
You warm, only the dream.
Freedom is a child you've got to sit with at night holding its hand,
When the pain rises and death laughs the blue laugh.
Freedom is a parable told by the old women who were always scrubbers
     of stone.
And the old women scrubbing stones
The rats gnawing the stones
Sharping their teeth on the stones
Freedom is a debt at the door and you've got to pay
And let the fire go out and the belly cackle.

The old women on their knees
The old men watching from the windows
The rats gnawing at the stones
Are you willing to creep through the wilderness
Hunchbacked with chains to grasp the dream, see the bird, climb the
     tower?

SLAVES:

Someday we're gonna tear them pillars down.
Someday these chains gonna rust an fertile the earth.

THE LEADER:
Are you willing to follow?

SLAVES:
Yes.

THE LEADER:
Do you swear by the dark hill the Saviour went,
By the chains you hold,
By the land you worked,
By the songs you sing,
By your children?

SLAVES:
Yes. YES.

THE LEADER:
Do you swear by the bird that's going to be flying in the new-uprising
      dawn?

SLAVES:
Yes, yes, YES, YES!

THE LEADER:
O follow in the dark and see the light,
Freedom's going to spring up out of the night.

SLAVES:
SOMEDAY WE'RE GONNA TEAR THEM PILLARS DOWN.

SAMUEL CHAPMAN ARMSTRONG

(Founder of Hampton Institute)

I

When he first came from Maui,
A Hawaiian island like a rainbow,
Soft and womanly island,
Tropical hosanna island,
The seasons were a circle of summers on that island.
There was peace there, quiet pools with golden fish,
Incredible soft green water and the coral leaning up.
America to him was no echo
Of his exotic world
Where volcanos made the people devout,
But a new raw world in itself:
Wilderness, wilderness blown by the west winds.

He saw America whole when he first came:
Paul Bunyan and the blue cow
Moving through the forests of the West, O Pioneers;
The Mississippi spending the land yearly with golden-ripe water;
New England quiet like a study and powerful like faith;
Georgia clay like dried blood;
The live oaks growing in Louisiana bayous like sorrow growing down;
Slaves bending over . . . and all the white cotton:
He saw when he first came.

II

He did what all men of his class did in their youth:
He went to college and was sheltered,
He was very serious and very gay.

When the Civil War slashed American air
For the first time visions lit his deep night sleep
Like so many candles lighting a night room.

He never dreamed half,
It was always the whole dream.
He never dreamed Present,
It was always the Future focus
Of sunlight on the Future.

He never saw East
Without the West;
He never spoke North
Without the South.
He was reasonable,
But he had visions,

Visions of dark free men
Making themselves free
Through the everlasting toil
That made them slaves.
Visions of free dark men,
Freed by song,
Gathering up toil with song,
Gathering respect with song,
Singing their way through darkness;
Visions of dark soldiers marching
Into battle with stripped sincerity
And always the songs singing into battle.

III

The dream was awake now
And he led first dark troops into battle
For their own freedom.

24

They sang as they had in his dream.
He had seen the Future even before he stood in that Present.
And in the Present he heard the Future singing.

The word was written on concrete paper:
Emancipation Proclamation: FREEDOM.
It rushed through the winter trees, dashed across mountains,
Flew in the air,
Men on horses rode by crying: FREEDOM!
The Ninth Regiment heard and rushed into prayer:
All those dark voices swept up tall like a pine
To God and the air was hallelujah with song,
The stars came out and freedom
Hung like a banner across the moon.

When the dark soldiers came back from prayer and song
They were in exultation;
Their eyes had felt the glory,
Their hands had touched a garment,
The deep river had been crossed,
The chariot swung low,
Millions of Daniels strode forth,
Pharaoh's army had been drowned:
All this was in their eyes.
They believed in miracles again
And Armstrong stood with them
With tears in his eyes.

He moved to them prophetic,
Ready to share their joy like broken bread at their communion,
Ready to drink their wine,
Knowing that the bread was broken and only represented,
Knowing that the wine would taste of blood.

IV

The Civil War was over
But his visions whispered:
It has only begun.
Then all the candles blew out
And he was awake with the morning.

He had been a General in War,
Now in Peace he would be a General fighting
Vice and ignorance and hate and prejudice
As if they were foes of cancer flesh and corrupt blood.

All over the South the freed dark men shouted: JUSTICE!
But the hanging oaks caught their words.
The dark voices cried: *Help us!* and their words
Fell between the Georgia clay like dried blood.
They moaned and their moaning settled in their hair—like fear.
Freedom was no different from their slavery,
Only the plantation where they could wander
Was a whole country now.
The chain marks were startling on their ankles,
The lash marks were startling on their backs,
They wandered the country setting their tents
Wherever the land was desolate and alone like themselves.

V

Now Armstrong knew that an altar must be built for their minds,
That their hands on plows, in soil, at bricks,
Must be wonderful to them, not sorrow.

So he was a General in Peace, fighting
Vice and ignorance and hate and decadence
As if they were foes of cancer flesh and terrible blood.

This school built from vision lighting vision,
From hope grown in a sour earth by him,
These new dark men and these new dark children,
These new dark women—this new race
All crescent America when this land flies danger signals at night.

VI

Now his name is monumental to us,
Not wholly in touchable things:
It is in the dignity of dark mothers;
In our sailors and soldiers when they sing like men of war;
It hovers over like permanent writing in our sky;
It holds some shine of the Peace to come;
It is an exultation to us here,
A constellation of optimistic stars
In the disaster volcanic in skies over free land.

MISS PACKARD AND MISS GILES

(Who founded Spelman College for Negro women in Georgia)

Two women, here in April, prayed alone
And saw again their vision of an altar
Built for mind and spirit, flesh and bone.

They never turned away, they never said
This dream is air, let us go back to our New England spring
And cultivate an earth that is not dead;

Let dark mothers weep, dark children bleed,
This land is barren land
Incapable of seed.

They made their crucifix far more
Than ornament; they wrestled with denial
And pinned him to the floor.

They made defeat an exile.
And year by year their vision shed its mist,
And still they smiled their Noah smile

Certain they had no death to fear,
Certain their future would be now
And all the Aprils we assemble here.

RAG DOLL AND SUMMER BIRDS

(For Frank Harriott)

I

We sit in our cabin corners waiting for God
And the stove goes out,
The newspapers on the walls, telling of crimes,
Curl away from the walls.

We wait for the doctor five miles away,
And the child under the rag covers whispers
To the rag doll and dies;
We wait and our bellies roar a declamation,
Tears speak from our eyes,
Scream to our hands held to our eyes.

We sit in our cabin corners
And the Bible is in the wind,
The songs we sing darken in the night,
The oil goes lower,
The lamp grows darker,
This darkness is not a tender darkness
The last moth leaves to fly
To light anotherwhere.
In the blackness the stars are not enough!

We sit in our cabin corners and the cabins blow away.

II

The snow cannot melt too soon for the birds left behind.
The crumbs fall in the crevices of snow

And the birds taste winter in their throats,
Wonder where the warm seasons went.
Their wings do not know the directions
The other flocks are gone, the signs are covered with winter.
There are no signals . . . Directionless . . . Lost . . . Alone . . .

Why are the flowers on the trees so white?
Why are these flowers so cold?

Smoke is in the chimneys where warmth is,
The sky is low and dark and level in the barns,
The intricate cobwebs are thinner than branches:
They are not singing places, not resting places,
Hay has not the smell of their nests,
Their songs turn to ice in the air.

The dark stiff little compact spots you see on these white fields are not
shadows.

THREE CHORUSES FROM
A VERSE DRAMA:
DIVINE COMEDY

DIVINE COMEDY

is about people in search of something
to believe in when they are trapped in
poverty, fear and prejudice. They follow a false prophet for a time, but when
he is killed, they turn to the strength
in themselves for guidance and faith.

WINTER CHORUS

BEFORE THE PROPHET CAME

(For Robert Elzy)

I

FIRST CHORUS:
Two winters come in one this year:
What crazy time is frozen in our hands?

SECOND CHORUS:
War and the least of war.

OLD MAN:
War ploughing seas for wet harvest,
Ploughing skies, wounding the moon,
Scything the stars.

CHORUS:
What crazy time is this?

OLD MAN:
Before is always now.
Before our hands froze,
Our ears, our membranes,
Before our blankets thinned
And our walls became unuseful against winter,

FIRST CHORUS:
Before all this, our hearts died
And the bitter juices were embalmed.

33

SECOND CHORUS:
All the sweetness drawn and spoiled.

FIRST CHORUS:
And the bitter juices embalmed.

ONE:
Yes, the world has been incredible for a long time.

CHORUS:
We have been obscene even to hopes of spring.
Poor and orderly we have been, poor and orderly.

ANOTHER:
The poor and the black seldom die early enough to be troublesome . . .

ANOTHER:
Or late enough.

FIRST CHORUS:
We go on like robot hands and feet
Or hieroglyphics marked in wet cement.

SECOND CHORUS:
Only the walking years will erase us
Or the pickax or the mechanical shovel with the automatic teeth.

FIRST CHORUS:
Cancel us.
Let doomsday come down
Like the foot of God on us.

SECOND CHORUS:
Be neat and swift
But be final.

34

CHORUS:
This time is our ghetto,
Black and hungry and spiritless.
Will we walk out of this time
Or limp out in the hunting season?

ONE:
We are clear and confused on many issues:
We are whole yet jointless;
We breathe and are breathless;
We bear children and are sterile;
We smile and the smile grins
As if it were cut into our faces.

GIRL:
I dance without legs.

ANOTHER GIRL:
I sing but my voice jars;
My mouth doesn't move!

CHORUS:
We are the poor who turn the granite wheel,
Blind and solid like Samson at Gaza revolving the wheel,
Some of us are black and the difference is apparent.

BLIND MAN:
The blind in the damp darkness
Without fire to warm the hands they've never seen,
What shall they do?

CHORUS:
Where is Christ?

ONE:
What crazy time is trembling in my hands?

ANOTHER:
Circus time with music running out.

ONE:
Where are the clowns?

CHORUS:
Despair,
Leaps in the air,
Falls down
Like a clown
I saw at a fair
Long, long ago.

BLIND MAN:
I want to see my hands
And the shape of this building I lean against.
What color is hair?
How are the Chinese different?
The black man?

ONE:
War, war will bomb your eyes open.

BLIND MAN:
Has a leper teeth?

ANOTHER:
War.

CHORUS:
For us.

ONE:
For all. For freedom.

36

ANOTHER:
The gangster: butcher war.

OLD MAN:
I knew slaughter once: saw it and kept my eyes shut for a week.
But shut, the slaughter repeated and repeated.

OLD WOMAN:
I remember slaughter too: there was blood:
After the last war that castrated the world,
Black soldiers came home to meet another foe
In the streets where they sang when they were boys.
And after the death and the shouting in Texas
Forty crazy women got down on their knees
And scrubbed the blood from out the streets
Till the pavement were clean as a prize elephant's skin.
When the blood came again they all had water on the knee.
And that was that.

ONE:
That wasn't that.
The blood was cancer deep—
Exhibit A to Z,
Neurotic blood in Texas.
When the rains shot accusing wetness
The blood came again
Original and hot.

GIRL:
There it is again. There. See it. See it there?

ANOTHER:
Where?

CHORUS:
Where?

ONE:
It's stuck to my feet.

ANOTHER:
I have it on my hands.

ONE:
There is no blood here,
Only in the olive groves of Italy.
The snow of Russia is stained,
Ethiopia has blood. England.
Some is left in Spain.
There are skinny kids in Poland.

CHORUS:
Will the blood come again?

ANOTHER:
To us here on our hands?

CHORUS:
Our blood or theirs?

ONE:
Both.

OLD MAN:
Blood is for dying men.
For the sick, the depleted.

CRAZY WOMAN:
White folks hate black folks
For sixty-three different reasons.
The wind is fierce here.

YOUNG MAN:
It's not that our feet are so cold,
Or that our clothes are imitations,
That we see the world cross-eyed, freedom and freedom reversed,
That the grandmother in the attic
Has lost her teeth as well as her gums . . .

BLIND MAN:
Has a leper teeth?

YOUNG MAN:
    . . . but the mirrors in this country are convex
And show our bodies distorted,
Are concave and show our minds hilarious.

CHORUS:
Where are the mirrors to show us normal
To pain
Love
Hate
Kindness?
To show we love our children?

CRAZY WOMAN:
We need a new star to live on.
The wind is fierce here.
I have rheumatism, arthritis, and cancer in my left armpit.
The wind is fierce here and my heart . . .

ONE:
Run before the wind slashes us altogether

ANOTHER:
Rip up the pavement and hide

ANOTHER:
Hide in the closets with automatic locks

ANOTHER:
Run into darkness for safety

ANOTHER:
Run to the attic

ANOTHER:
The cellar

ANOTHER:
Run!!!

OLD MAN:
If you run, the city hounds are faster,
The country hounds are more practiced.
Stand here and lean against each other.

CHORUS:
Cancel us,
Let doomsday come down
Like the foot of God on us.

MOTHER:
Singing to her baby and then humming.
Sleep, darling, sleep,
Sleep, darling, sleep.
There will be milk in the morning and bread,
There will be blankets to cover your bed.
Sleep, darling, sleep.
There will be toys to play with and keep.
Sleep, darling, sleep,
Sleep, darling, sleep.

MOTHERS:
What shall we do with our children asleep,
Dreaming the promise we never can keep?

40

YOUNG MAN:
That lullaby will not soothe us.
Nothing like music will warm us.
We are used to music,
We used it eighty years.
The lullaby will not cheer the black baby.

CRAZY WOMAN:
Already it knows the wind is real fierce here.

OLD MAN:
It is true we cannot smile or sing into freedom.

BLIND MAN:
What color is hair?

CRAZY WOMAN:
The longer we wait,
The shorter we'll be dead.

CHORUS:
Where is Christ?
Where is Christ?

BLIND MAN:
He's hanging on the cross
Dripping blood again.
There's a sharp crown again;
He's seeing blood, only blood
In front of his eyes.

ONE:
Where have you seen this?

BLIND MAN:
I know all about the look of crucifixion.

41

ONE:
Christ is waiting in the church for us.

YOUNG MAN:
We don't seek food so much,
Or shelter; there are still floors to scrub,
Brass to shine, tables to wait upon.
That is mostly what we do and we do it.

CHORUS:
We need hope. Where can we go?

ONE:
To the rulers.
Come on.

II

*The people have assembled in a church. When the Priest finishes
    making a sign of the cross:*

YOUNG MAN:
We come asking for simple hope,
Iron for our spirits in a limping time.
We wish liberty and peace and freedom.
We have seen the blue flame of death
Lighting our streets,
The spider in the cradle,
Brotherhood in a straitjacket,
Our men denied because they are black,
Our children neurotic.
Now we are afraid and alone.
Where is our Master, Christ?

PRIEST:

Christ is here and in your homes,
Go home now and pray.
Take the dusty hymnal down from the dusty shelf.
Polish the silver rosary again,
Re-set the crooked cross,
Re-clothe the naked Christ.
Go back to your homes and light the flameless candle.

YOUNG MAN:

We have been lighting little candles for long, too long.
Now we need the big light of the sun.
Where is Christ?
A crazy time is delivered into our hands.
We cannot drop it or cancel it or ignore it.

CHORUS:

What shall we do?

PRIEST:

The Lord's children are never alone or angry.
Prayer changes things. Go home and pray.

CHORUS:

We have prayed in the solid night,
But still our children rub their skin in terror
And stare at their hands.
There are faces at our windows,
Nooses in our hallways.

PRIEST:

Go home and pray.

CHORUS:

We have no home!

As the Priest starts to leave:

ONE:
Don't go away.
Please—there's the blue light of death
In our streets . . .

ANOTHER:
. . . Death in the air.

ANOTHER:
Two winters in one this year.

PRIEST:
Christ will comfort you.

CHORUS:
Where is Christ?

YOUNG MAN:
There's an acetylene torch
Tracing promises on my chest.

ONE:
On mine.

ANOTHER:
And mine.

CHORUS:
Hypocrisy!

PRIEST:
Go home and pray.

CHORUS:
Terror!

44

PRIEST:
Go home and pray.

CHORUS:
Bigotry!
Lust!

PRIEST:
Go home and pray.

CHORUS:
Hatred!

PRIEST:
Go home and pray.

CHORUS:
We cannot go home when blood leaks
Down the gutters and cannot be drained:
When scrubbing is folly and acid is vain.
We cannot go home. We have no home.
The children are weeping.

ONE MOTHER:
Stop the children weeping.

FIRST CHORUS:
What crazy time is this?
Where is Christ?

SECOND CHORUS:
Let doomsday come down
Like the foot of God on us.

YOUNG MAN:
Incense won't heal my chest.
Where shall I turn?

BLIND MAN:
Has a leper teeth?
Where shall I turn?

YOUNG GIRL:
There's water in the river.

YOUNG BOY:
I'm so black they call me nighttime.
When I walk along everyone looks for stars.

FIRST CHORUS:
Where shall we turn?

SECOND CHORUS:
Call up the government on the telephone.

MOTHER: *Singing*
Sleep, darling, sleep.
Sleep, darling, sleep.
There will be milk in the morning and bread,
There will be blankets to cover your bed.
Sleep, darling, sleep.

MOTHERS:
What shall we do with our children asleep,
Dream. . . .

MOTHER: *Singing*
Sleep, darling, sleep
Sleep, darl—
Mother realizing that she is holding a dead child

Burn the blanket,
My baby has died.

MOTHERS: *Moaning*
Her baby is dead, dead, dead . . .

YOUNG MAN:
I knew the year spring never came,
Summer or harvest never grew
I witnessed in person the year when winter was dictator
And the trees disappeared in favor of ice.

OLD MAN:
I knew the year when the birds froze
In the climate of their usual resort.

ONE:
Boil seeds instead of onions.

ANOTHER:
Rescue last year's potatoes from the bin.

ANOTHER:
The rats have the wheat. Corner them!

OLD MAN:
I knew the year when two winters came,
When I planted coal in the furnace
I reaped the frozen air

YOUNG MAN:
Explain that miracle and concentrate
On the growing fingernails of this dead infant.

MOTHER:
Jesus, find us again.

CHORUS:
Where is Christ?

CRAZY WOMAN: *Whispering*
I hear a new Christ.

YOUNG BOY:
When I walk along the streets
I hear white voices out of white faces and white eyes,
They whisper and shout . . .

VOICES:
You are black, you are black,
You are dangerously black.

CHORUS:
Where is Christ?

CRAZY WOMAN:
White folks hate black folks
For sixty-three different reasons.

OLD MAN:
There is violence and terrible in the air.

CHORUS: *Whispering*
Where is Christ?
Where is Christ?

STAR CHORUS
THE COMING OF THE PROPHET

(*For Winifred Daboll*)

MESSENGER:
We have heard from whisperings running on the wind,
From gossip belched out by reliable tongues,
From miracles performed without the usual wand
And basic contraptions . . .
From the fat look of hitherto skinny faces,
That a prophet has come,
A protector,
A giver of food.

SECOND CHORUS:
What was whispered we have not heard,
For the wind only howls in our ears.
What miracles?
What gossip?
The tongues we hear bring only heartbreak for a song
And the eyes we have seen have been skinny and haunted and bloody.

ONE:
Where is this protector,
How can we find him?

SECOND CHORUS:
Claim him,
Have food and a light for guidance?
Where is this deliverer to deliver us
From hate and prejudice?

49

MESSENGER:

It has been said that Christ has forsaken
The angels, left them to their flutes and their wings
And their heaven-pearly-gate songs.

ANOTHER:

He has raced down miles of time
To walk among us again.
He has brushed past stars,
His robe glitters with stars.

FIRST CHORUS:

Where is this man with a robe of stars?
Where is this deliverer?
Where is this Christ?

OLD WOMAN

Seeing our misery He has come to us.
He is walking right here on earth
Giving out pieces of Heaven
If we'll only believe in Him
And claim Him again.

MESSENGER:

He brings light,
He brings light.

CHORUS:

Where shall we find Him who comes again
As He said He would ages back
When He ruled only half of the earth
Where?

SOME:

We are winter worn,
Is there a new star to guide us to Him?

CHORUS:

We have forgotten the look of the Bethlehem star
That shone on an easier world,
Warmer world,
A fig-tree
Golden frankincense world.
Where is the new star?

YOUNG MAN

Let us seek like shepherds in modern rags,
Let us find the star.

CHORUS:

Let us all seek.

MOTHER:

Seek, seek, all of you, seek.
He comes too late by half a week.
Burn the blanket.
Let it be forgotten
My baby has died.

ANOTHER:

My boy was six feet tall and wonderful,
Now he's six feet down and dead.

YOUNG MAN:

It is the living now, the living.
Let the dead be warm in the earth,
Let the earth be warm on the dead.
Reconsider your dead,
Consider them dead.

ONE:

Every wound must heal or fester
Every past must pass away.

CHORUS:
Which is the shelter star?
Which is His star?
We have waited long
Wandered far
Into misery looking for this star.
Now when it comes we cannot choose.

BLIND MAN:
I have never seen a star.
I look up to darkness always;
Guide me to this shelter star.

YOUNG MAN:
Why do we wait?
Why do we hesitate?
Let us find this Christ
Who sends this sign.

ONE:
Come on!
You who are left in red rain
With pain
In your bones.

ANOTHER:
You who feel death
Like a breath
On your hands, come on!

ANOTHER:
You who have no freedom
Relinquish freedom.
Come on.

ANOTHER:
I have heard my children cry for food
In the night,
I will follow this light.

BLIND MAN:
Don't leave the blind to wander
Where the wind is a wall!

YOUNG MAN:
Why do we wait?
Why do we hesitate?

PRIEST:
The saints you pray to will hear
In spite of the long-coming answer,
And the dull winter will turn
Back to autumn again.
Return to prayer,
Return to the saints and their blessing.

CHORUS:
Do you know what hunger is?
Do you know what terror is?
Do you know the slow-crawling agony of color?

MOTHER:
Have you seen the dead child without a coffin?
Have you watched the mother's eyes?

YOUNG MAN:
Don't trace the cross in the air;
Rip off your lace, rip it to thread.
Sell your images for us,
Mortgage the church for us.

Let your brass constellations tarnish.
Go down.

CHORUS:
You are not worthy.
Grow fat!

YOUNG MAN:
Grow rich!

CHORUS:
But go down!

PRIEST: *They begin to move off*
How can I bring light
If you thrust His chalice from my hand?
You follow a false prophet,
Stare at false miracles.
Desert His name and blow the candles out.
You are not worthy.

YOUNG MAN
As long as our bellies are empty
We will follow any God,
We would pawn the halo about the head of Christ,
Unhaunt the Ghost
Who knows the secret:
The turning of stone to bread,
Of water to wine,
Despair to hope,
Black to white!

PRIEST:
You must wait; be tested.

They all are gone

54

AUTUMN CHORUS

AFTER THE PROPHET HAS BEEN KILLED

(For Allardyce Nicoll)

YOUNG MAN
What comet was ever a star again?
Look to your nights when one star burns
Brighter than all the rest,
Burns out of its place
And falls like a vertical fan of light
Shooting through the night
And into the earth.
The end of its burning is stone,
The end of its glory is stone,
The end is always stone.

THOSE AROUND BODY:
He said He has no end.

YOUNG MAN:
Wipe his awful memory from your lips,
Wipe the blunt horror from your eyes,
Thumb your ears against the swift bullet sound.
Remember he is dead and you are here.

BLIND MAN:
The blind in the haunted places,
Having heard destruction and death,
Will go back to a year of two winters
Without fire to warm the hands they never saw.

THOSE AROUND BODY: *Chanting*
He said He would not die.
This is the test,

55

We must win as the years move by, lest
He look down from the sky
On those He blest
To find them gone away.

Do not let your hair down,
Do not put the sackcloth on,
Now that He has gone.

Wrap the body in stone
Lay it bone for bone
In the tomb.

He left it here for us to keep.
He left it here to guard our sleep,
To guard our faith,
So do not weep.

Golgotha, Golgotha
Death on a windy hill,
The winter wind is crying
Down the ages still,

Golgotha, Golgotha,
Upon a windy slope,
Where Mary loosed her hair
Abandoning hope,

We feel your wind,
But our eyes are dry
Because we know
He cannot die.

Wrap the body in stone
Lay it bone for bone
In the tomb.

YOUNG MAN:
Turn to yourselves!

YOUNG GIRL:
Turn to ourselves? We are empty and broken.
Laden with grief that cannot be spoken.

OLD WOMAN:
Once we were flying.

YOUNG GIRL:
Not high—

OLD WOMAN:
But flying—

OLD MAN:
The birds have been shot and their wings have been closed.

YOUNG GIRL:
Oh, it is better to lie in the winter again
Like grounded birds, like stricken men.

CHORUS: *Negro*
And still we thrive, lie close to earth;
Grounded birds, are healed and live again:
Anointed at our birth with dark water,
Bidden to crawl like worms—sliced or broken.
Still like worms we live with a dearth
Of stars and more soil than we can eat.

Can we repeat
The legends of three hundred years:
The fears,
The terrors,

57

The broken moons,
The fallen jungle stars?

Still we thrive, lying close to earth
With mirth
For a constellation,
And no elation
But a zig-zag music
Shimmering through our blood,
And after that the pains
Of a spirit ticking itself away,
And flesh rotting to clay,
Rotting our day.

CHORUS: *White*
And still we thrive, lie close to earth,
Grounded birds, are healed and live again.
Anointed at our birth with crystal water,
Bidden to part the earth communion bread among us
From the start.
We are the man underfoot, too.
The same as you.

ALL:
What shall we do?

YOUNG MAN:
This shall not be forever.
The black hand matching the black hand,
The white hand matching the black hand,
The hands that stab the machines to churning,
The hands that plant the corn,
Hands at battle,
Endless hands of yearning,
Hands that question:

These will wave a banner like a signal of faith
To flesh the bony army of the poor.

OLD WOMAN:
"To flesh the bony army of the poor."
He gave you the way of bread for a time
But you need the way of freedom too:
The stir in your hearts that makes the days
Even the dark days, sweet to live.
I come to you an old woman in the twelfth month of the year,
In the twelfth month of my days.
I come like any old black woman who has had to carry
The dark weight of living on her breast.
I have seen sharp days with anger in the gutters,
Hope crucified and lonely there,
I have seen my little girl tramped on,
Felt my hand broke, lost God,
My best friend shout for joy and die,
My boy kill for all of us.
I know, Lord, I know the deep well side of life.
O listen, you poor and forgotten and you of little faith.
Pray to that cross, cause when you pray to it,
You pray to the Christ in you that stood against a great big hill of pain.
I'm ashes, and you can't light ashes
But you are great hunks of coal
And you can burn when the kindling is put to you.
You are free to attempt freedom,
My son said this as goodbye.
You are the power in Christ,
Christ is the power in you,
The power and the glory.

CHORUS:
We feel no Christ, no power in His cross.
We feel our strength now, but not His power and strength.

Tell us, leader,
Where is this Christ in us?
Where is this Christ in us in this new winter?

The old woman spoke in riddles.
Spoke of her pain and her death and her ashes.
Now in the time of our uniting, where is our Master, Christ?
The hope we forsook for common bread?
The Saint who fled His Father's house to die for us?
Where is He?

YOUNG MAN:
He is the new strength you feel;
He has clasped the burning hand of autumn
And led the harvest into this winter.
He was the far-off dream of your uniting.
He is the dream made real,
The pain made courage,
The hope made living.
He is yourselves when you throw off the sackcloth of submission.
When you wipe the begging eye of tears.

CHORUS:
He is ourselves when we throw off the sackcloth of submission,
When we wipe the begging eye of tears.
Christ has clasped the burning hand of autumn
And led a ripened harvest to our door.
The earth is not barren this winter,
The autumn burns through this winter.
The leaves are still red,
The streams are still free:
This harvest is harvest for every tree.

YOUNG MAN:
We have fled back to autumn,
We have shed winter for autumn.

This mystic hope in prophets has turned
To a firmer hope in our hearts.
The deserted places have burned
And from them our Phoenix departs,
Rises up and flies in our lands,
Uniting our hands,
Uniting our faith.

SEMI-CHORUS:
We need no prophets

SEMI-CHORUS:
This winter is autumn

SEMI-CHORUS:
We need no miracles

SEMI-CHORUS
We are the miracles

ALL:
We are the earth itself.

POEMS FOR MY BROTHER

KENNETH

I

I remember from your life: the senior laughter,
The senior laughter and the big stain
Death marked on the pillow where you died;
How the morning shadows came to hide
The bed
Where you lay—dead;
The horizontal smooth patterns of the maple coffin.

Later nights I dreamt you awoke
And took me by the hand
To the hall
Of the grave
And gave
Me duties to perform when I went out.
That was all.

Duties like remembering how to sit
Laughing at life by being part of it;
Like knitting long threads of laughter
To blanket the silence in the hall, Hereafter.

And I said: Is there some way to watch long tanks creep
Over the world with their iron sound and still sleep?
When the dark body of the ruined dark boy
Is ashes and bones, how can I talk with joy?

There was no reply:
You gave me a smile and returned to the grave.

Our country will not be in war again:
A mock-war played by children who dreamt of soldiers
And soldiers' houses in the earth,
Of banners and the great burning splash of rainbow shells
Drying the earth, the toy dead lying stiff
Staring their painted stare.
Immediate resurrection: the game was on again.
It was only a child war then!

III

Suddenly all the voices stopped,
Suddenly as you would blow a candle out
Or click the radio off,
The transmission ended;
The concert was over for the night.
I would hear again,
The announcer said,
In the morning . . . *the morning* . . .

IV

My chief citizen is dead
And my town at half-mast:
Even in speech,
Even in walking,
Even in seeing
The busy streets where he stood
And the room where he was host to his friends
And his enemies, where we erased the night to dawn
With conversation of what I had seen and he had seen

And done and written during the space of time we were apart.
We will not talk again with common breath.
His voice has gone to talk to death.
There is a new language to learn
And I am learning like a truant child.
I do not understand this code, this life to death.
I will not be convinced that we must
Only talk again as dust to dust.

v

If we had counted all the stars
And made each constellation clear,
I'd recognize more than this spear
Swinging from the solid side of Mars.

But when we went, not long ago
Exploring all that silver land,
I would not stay because the snow
Turned ice within my hand.

vi

Your memory is my star and my night.
The two shine contrapuntally, their music
I read in sounds, I read in listening:
All the pretensions we once thought so bright.

I knew you in the early days before
The words for freedom rang on stone,
And the high terrible sign of truth
Was all we wished and all we saw.

The vocabulary belongs to you now dead,
Whose language was deeper than life
And wider than the curve of sea
We scanned from this beach before this came instead.

My heart has no fountains to reach in air
To what was pure and singing in our life;
The music fountains stay below the earth,
And bomb-dust fountains burst truth everywhere.

VII

Sleep late with your dream.
The morning has a scar
To mark on the horizon
With the death of the morning star.

The color of blood will appear
And wash the morning sky,
Aluminum birds flying with fear
Will scream to your waking,
Will send you to die;

Sleep late with your dream.
Pretend that the morning is far,
Deep in the horizon country,
Unconcerned with the morning star.

VIII

Death, split-second guest, negative magician
When will you believe you are not final?
After you have touched a heart
And tricked it into silence,

Standing smooth and quiet by your side,
Memory robs you,
Picks your pockets clean,
Then rings her bells
And dances with the years.
Chemistry-master Death, mourn for yourself,
Mourn for your sad-Judas-wandering occupation,
Mourn for your swift silences, your stiffness,
Your company of worms,
Mourn for your own life, Death.

That body in the ground
With the chin set hard against the neck
Expanding the face,
The rigid shoulders,
The hands posed artificially,
Is awaiting nothing—
It has its final horizontal home.

Even though the sun comes only through the roots
Like vitamins, it does not matter.
There will be no resurrection: no eager Gabriel trumpet.
The resurrection is now, in Memory
Ringing all her jester bells;
Is now and for the ever of all my days.

IX

Here is holly for you, brother, here is mistletoe,
Here is the song we sing this Christmas with the cold sparrow.

We come with Christmas in our arms on the day of the original Child,
But woven in these blanket wreaths is sorrow, pared and wild.

It is almost a year now, nearing the twentieth day
Of the second month, when you died, so we will lay

Holly with berries, and hemlock washed and clean
For the earth to celebrate with us what you have been.

ALL THIS REVIEW

COUNTEE CULLEN

(1903-1946)

Now begins the sleep, my friend:
Where the cold dirt blanket is, you will be warm,
Where seeds begin to root, you will flower.
The dilapidation of our earth is left for us to order.
Your heart that was strong will help us carry
Whatever trouble springs to hunch our backs,
Whatever anger grows to sty our eyelids,
Whatever unexpected happiness comes like hope to smile our lips
—We would be ugly now except for hope.

Now begins the sleep, my friend:
You showed us that men could see
Deep into the cause of Lazarus,
Believe in resurrection.
You come back to us
Not unwinding a shroud and blinking at known light
But singing like all the famed birds,
Nightingale, lark and nightjar.
You come back to us with the truth
Of your indignation, protest and irony.
Also in your brave and tender singing
We hear all mankind yearning
For a new year without hemlock in our glasses.

WHEN I AM DEAD

Now would I tread my darkness down
And wish for clover overhead;
The roots below will twine a crown
When I am dead.

The seal of color stamps too deep
For wounded flesh to live and win;
The earth is shielding and will keep
My darkness close within.

CIRCLE ONE

(For Gordon Heath)

Nothing happens only once,
Nothing happens only here,
Every love that lies asleep
Wakes today another year.

Why we sailed and how we prosper
Will be sung and lived again;
All the lands repeat themselves,
Shore for shore and men for men.

75

CIRCLE TWO

O, I been travelin over all,
I been to Maine and Tennessee,
Arkansas an New Orleans,
Ain't nothing new nowhere to see.

Everywhere I go the same,
The same ole land to dig an sow,
Love winkin dressed in scarlet red,
Dancin in an out the do.

ENGAGEMENT

If there must be elaborate favors
For this simple partnership of years,
Elaborate whisperings in the fragrant ear,
Kissing by the hour and by the letter,
Accounts of how the evening went
When I went out alone,
Where this dollar disappeared and where the small affection
Like the ear kiss
If each time you catch my eye mine must twinkle back:
"I love you and will through thick and thin,
Especially through the thick, my dear, especially then . . ."
If I must arrange my letters so that I can tell
Which have been touched or re-arranged by kettle steam,
If I must thread my needle with the camel
Of your curiosity, explore the haystack,
Unload the woodpile . . .
Then no and no and no.

I have other fish to fry over other fires
In the meadows of another country.

MIDNIGHT BELL

This cannot be the hour for oral speech:
Words vying with the wind, with private sounds
Of other lovers striving on the beach,
With waves: the sand sniffers, the hounds.
No, this is quiet in between the long
Sentences, the lengths of speech at will.
Let the eyes remember, the ears catch the songs
We sing deep in the bone, in the still
Unoutward parts, that have their resurrection
In themselves. Cancel the mouth of poetry and prose;
Be eager now to seek the dark confection
In the flesh and feed until desire goes,
Until we sleep, until we cannot tell
Why midnight walked and did not ring her bell.

DRUNKEN LOVER

This is the stagnant hour:
The dead communion between mouth and mouth,
The drunken kiss lingered,
The dreadful equator south.

This is the hour of impotence
When the unfulfilled is unfulfilled.
Only the stale breath is anxious
And warm. All else is stilled.

Why did I come to this reek,
This numb time, this level?
Only for you, my love, only for you
Could I endure this devil.

I dreamed when I was
A pimply and urgent adolescent
Of these hours when love would be fire
And you the steep descent.

My mouth's inside is like cotton,
Your arm is dead on my arm.
What I pictured so lovely and spring
Is August and fungus calm.

O lover, draw away, grow small, go magic,
O lover, disappear into the tick of this bed;
Open all the windows to the north
For the wind to cool my head.

IGNORE THOSE SEALS

The new year beckons with a crooked finger:
All I have left at the moment to remember
Is several hours when thoughts were numb
In a deformed solitude the last of December.

That was because we drank too much,
Understanding the common falsehood,
The intellectual fraud, the meant deception,
The snatches of terror, more than we should.

The fire was warm and delicious in the room,
Tall shadows of our loneliness
Made calm over the restless, over the hot odors
Of passion in the biting kiss.

Now we must face it even with the curtains drawn,
While the wind is like prosecution at the panes,
While your eyelids twitch, your knuckles crack,
While outside the actual storm remains.

Look at me now and do not regret, but awake
To the new year's contempt for regret
And the old year's notarized epitaphs.
Ignore those seals, my love. Forget.

ALL THIS REVIEW

I loved you when we were young
But pity when you are old
The letters you carry, the poems
Where years ago I told

How the hour would arrive
(Your hair already grey)
When you would touch these papers
And look miles away

To now as I write these words
Saying I long for you
At four in the morning, at nine:
All this review.

When any condition prevails
In sleep or in awake
I see your constellation eyes
Shine while my senses take

Morning to breathe—and smother,
Hope to sing—and sorrow,
Sun—an enchanted sieve
Shedding rain tomorrow.

I shape you in my fingers,
Cover you in that rain,
Carry you like a bright toy
To Christmas air again.

But I am lonely and startled,
Rain repeats tears to me,
The toy grows bored,
Sends away the child, amuses itself with the tree.

You are afraid of my celebration,
Draw my passion to dust like a game,
Gather every bauble
To scar with your name.

Pity the letters and you in the poems,
But never pity me.
That toy is grey and tarnished
Under that Christmas tree.

THE VERDICT

There is no evidence current that you loved me,
Or witnesses: there was fire for the letters,
And those I told are promised, sealed.

Once there was a prism even the sun
Could not glory, light came from
Somewhere more abstract than the sky.

But light is the name, there is no other;
This light was human living, not aerial,
Mixed, fragrant, showing even at blazing noon,

Never in a dark so solid nothing
Struck through: sun or star or moon
Or artificial lamp, electric-full.

It is no secret: the somewhere light was you,
Not the flesh part only, not the bone part merely
But the dream undyed with passion:

You when there was no henceforth
To walk, no now to penetrate,
No therewas to shadow. You in clarity.

The prism still lies near the clock,
But time nestling up to dawn, to spring in afternoon,
Loves hours, only hours, never light.

I BREAK THE SKY

Only the deep well
With its reflecting echo
Knows the long dismay
I call this afternoon.

Because my voice is downward
Leaning over shale and torture rock
Surrounding the narrow of this well,
Nothing hears as I cry your name.

There are trees,
The birds they nest are deaf;
All the animals have rejected
The emotion my echo mourns.

Far, far down, the end is prepared
In the sky that breaks as I fall.
I see my face coming, foreshorted descent,
The whiz, the slime—and the sky is whole.

THAT STAR

Regard the first star
As the warning and the call:
Although I am as mortal
As Christmas in war,
Yet I will light whenever
It is evening and your eye
Looks to that sky
Where love burns, surety.

Therefore, whenever day is low,
(Remember always, and forget
Whenever trivia beset you)
Glance upward and convince
Your third eye that I am there
Lighting downward to your heart
With my own lantern.

I am not proud or overhot;
Whoever loves knows this:
We all are subject to the kiss
Of those we love, of those.

THE REUNION

I loved the apple-sweetness of the air
And pines that settled slanting on the hill,
Indians old and soft with needles there,
Where once we stood, and both so strangely still.
We must have surely known what other days
Would come in other flaming autumn's flame.
And even though we walk through different ways
To different hills that hill remains the same.
Watch every splendor, envy all the sky,
But recognize the days we knew, and hear
The simple sounds we heard. As birds that fly
Southward to warmth, we shall come back one year.
The little teeth of time will make no mark
On any stone, on any leaf or bark.

COUNTERPOINT

JONATHAN'S SONG

A NEGRO SAW THE JEWISH PAGEANT,
"WE WILL NEVER DIE"

(For Sol Gordon)

I am a part of this:
Four million starving
And six million dead:
I am flesh and bone of this.

I have starved
In the secret alleys of my heart
And died in my soul
Like Ahab at the white whale's mouth.

The twisted cross desire
For final annihilation
Of my race of sufferers:
I am Abel, too.

Because my flesh is whole
Do not think that it signifies life.
I am the husk, believe me.
The rest is dead, remember.

I am a part of this
Memorial to suffering,
Militant strength:
I am a Jew.

Jew is not a race
Any longer—but a condition.

All the desert flowers have thorns;
I am bleeding in the sand.

Take me for your own David:
My father was not cruel,
I will sing your psalms,
I have learned them by heart.

I have loved you as a child,
We pledged in blood together.
The union is not strange,
My brother and my lover.

There was a great scent of death
In the garden when I was born.
Now it is certain:
Love me while you can.

The wedding is powerful as battle,
Singular, dread, passionate, loud,
Ahab screaming and the screaming whale
And the destination among thorns.

Love is a triple desire:
Flesh, freedom, hope:
No wanton thing is allowed.
I will sing thy psalms, all thy psalms,
Take me while you can.

CONVERSATION ON V

"They got pictures of V stamped on letter stamps;
Miss Eagle wear one in her lapel to her Red Cross suit;
Mr. Bigful, the bank president, got one in his lapel too;
Some of the people I do laundry with got great big ones in they
      windows;
Hadley Brothers Department Store uptown got pictures of V on they
      store-bought dresses,
Even got a V ice-cream dish—girls selling them so fast had to run up
      a sign: NO MORE V SUNDAES;
And bless God, Lucy done gone up North and come back with one
      gleaming on her pocketbook.
Now let's get this straight: what do them V's mean?"
"V stands for Victory."
"Now just what is this here Victory?"
"It what we get when we fight for it."
"Ought to be Freedom, God do know that!"

WEDDING POEM FOR JOSEPH AND EVELYN JENKINS

Now the thunder is real in the sky
And birds are not birds that fly
Through artificial lightning, humming hysterical music,
Gleaming in a supernatural sun,
Ignoring the children, the lovers, the sick,
As they open their bowels to below
And death like a silver bullet
Splits the air and falls below.
Beautiful and modern and fierce,
Singing evil and death, they strike
All living with a kind of doomsday destruction:
Burying children's toys, old men's memories, women's rings;
Burying the cradle as well as the throne.

Strange how impersonal the battle seems
Although it will have a personal history
To everything from the rat gnawing the floor
To the children who sing crazy but will no more.

Strange how a garden yields from seeds
But in between the flowers the weeds will grow like evil
Without an apparent concrete signal:
Strong, treacherous, fertile, dull.

But there is other music in the earth harmonious in the garden and
the jail:
The love of man for woman, the worth

Of children they will make, the coming spring,
The clear eye of hope too is an everlasting thing.

Is it incredible that love is stronger than bridges,
Can outguess the intuition of the fox,
Can make the boiling alleys in the moon
Visible and the night collapse too soon?

Every war is a condition of love:
Love for gold in the pocket
Or land in another land,
Or liberty where you stand.

But the marriage of hearts is highest in the scale,
Most difficult note to hear.
The lungs must breathe a pure air
To send the note with clarity anywhere.

When the mind records on its hard metal
This music, plays it again and again
Until the heart is satisfied
That all hate has died,

Then the thunder and the heartless birds
Will be vaguer than mist,
Then you will be able to walk in danger
Knowing death is false,
That all sound and sight
But one voice and one face
Are a stranger.

IPHIGENIA

(*For Ednah Bethea*)

Out of the sin of man
Comes the sin of mankind,
And we are corroded,
We are corroded, O my dear.

I have looked for summer
And found only bareness,
Blank bareness in the trees,
Bareness, bareness
And another season stripped, O my dear.

Health is for our children only:
The syphilis of this time
Eats away the fulness
The fulness and the mercy, O my dear.

We are on the altar,
Sacrificial and elect
To feel the steady knife:
The knife unshaped by us, but the knife:
The final spilling, O my dear.

Credit the past with indecencies,
Let them be museum to the future.
We will be dead in our horizontal death
But say we shared in the future
By this spilling blood
And this death on the altar,
O my dear.

We will die but we are innocent.
Go to the records, read the cause,
Sandpaper the sky to erase the blood.
Doomsday will shed doomsday
On those who deal another destruction
From another sky:
O my dear, O my dear, O my dear.

THE DECISION

Who are these among you
Homesick for home, longing for peace—
The summer going and the war going
And all the sharp promises of peace?

Watch from your foxholes
For fire on distant mountains,
Fire flags lit with peace
Waving on the mountains.

There are other journeys
You must make after your journey home,
Other journeys you must make alone
Into the countries of the heart
To sit with silence and decide alone

If your final home will be
Where brother knows brother,
Chews meat, breaks bread
Together with his brother;

Or where a man will trample again
His neighbor, shake no hands,
Scorn fellowship, light fires
Of dark bones and flesh to warm his hands.

Who are these among you
Longing for peace among all men,
Longing for each homesick heart
To make a pilgrimage among all men?

COUNTERPOINT

(For Carl Van Vechten)

Terror does not belong to open day

Picnics on the beach, all along
The unmined water children play,
A merry-go-round begins a jingle song,
Horses churn up and down the peppermint poles,
Children reach for the brassy ring,
Children laugh while the platform rolls
Faster and faster while the horses sing:

merry-ro, merry-o,
this is the way your lives should go:
up and down and all around
listening to this merry sound.

Terror does not belong to open day

merry-ro, merry-ha,
snatch this ring and plant a star;
grow a field of magic light,
reap it on a winter night.

Terror does not belong to open day

THE WATCHING

And Samson cried out terrified and afraid,
He bit the long hair at his lower lip,
Massaged his chin with a sleeping hand.
While the woman watched Samson began to weep.
The pink of his fingernails turned the color of ripe olives
And carefully his eyes opened to slits:
Asleep in his dream but awake in his intimations,
He dreamed his head would be harvest for a scythe and a woman.
The woman watched.
Tears paused in his eyes as he slept his dangerous sleep.

DEFINITION

(For Louisa Leftwich)

Everyone says: fate is a bad number,
Should be jailed and put on bread and water.
Fate has drilled into the spirit's bone,
And all our marrow has leaked out.

They talk of fate as they talk of God and Devil;
Something like a storm between mountains
Or tigers or whales or tornadoes,
Something like the chemistry of air.

Fate is ourselves awake and asleep,
Fighting in the sky or armies in the earth,
Speeches, treaties, elections, hopes of heaven,
Preparations for hell. Fate is the collection plate

Of our sins and our loves—variety of coins,
Stored away or stolen by those fakirs
Who blame the plus or minus of our condition
On God or Devil or the sound of the sea.

THE PRECEDENT

(For the Riesers)

There are still birds,
They have not all been killed;
They wander lost in the smoke,
The nests distorted, the eggs broken:
This they have not willed.

They still have the air
But the grass is not the same.
There are giants stalking
Where grasshoppers jumped.
What is their name?

The giants are man,
My swallow, my robin,
Their prey is the earth
But the flower you see
In the moss will win.

Eventually the broken tree
Will be restored again
And the songs will cut the smoke
With sweetness, and all will
Prosper with men.

When and how is secret
Like the egg, but know
My birds, that seasons have
A precedent: spring will come
Like fire to the snow.

MARTHA GRAHAM

Seek, seek the dream,
Pursue the dream awake:
In an underneath hunt
That makes the heart break.

There is the world chasing the world
In the dark, in the spaceless dark
While the moon hides terrified
At the mechanical cannon bark.

Into the dark and into the light
The more you dance in the dark;
Dance your way to wisdom
And dance out with the spark.

The neurotic, the foxhole soldier,
The king with a damp crown,
The housewife, the lonesome sister,
And those who have lost their way:
Dance them out of the speechless dark
Into the talking day.

We hardly knew but now we know
The angular pattern of the puritan mind
And the puritan pattern the curious curve
Bends over to find.

Man's body is the music and the soul,
And where the dream is perfect, ugly or mean,

The tents of his hope are lifted
And even the tainted raised clean,

Even when the world is chasing the world
In an Alice-in-Wonderland fable of fear,
Remember us, remember us,
And dance, dance near, dance near. . . .

OPEN LETTER

Brothers, let us discover our hearts again,
Permitting the regular strong beat of humanity there
To propel the likelihood of other terror to an exit.

For at last it is nearly ended: the daily anguish needles
Probing in our brains when alarms crust the air
And planes stab over us.

(Tears screamed from our eyes,
Animals moaned for death, gardens were disguised,
Stumps strained to be whole again.)

For at last it is nearly ended, grass
Will be normal, hillsides
Pleased with boys roaming their bellies.

All the mourning children
Will understand the long word, hallelujah,
Each use for joy will light for them.

The torn souls and broken bodies will be restored,
Primers circulate for everlasting peace,
The doors to hope swung open.

Brothers, let us enter that portal for good
When peace surrounds us like a credible universe.
Bury that agony, bury this hate, take our black hands in yours.